THRIVING AND BLACK

THE PLAYBOOK

DEANNAH STINSON REESE

3G Publishing, Inc.
Loganville, Ga 30052
www.3gpublishinginc.com
Phone: 1-888-442-9637

First published by 3G Publishing, Inc. February, 2021.

ISBN: 9781941247860

Printed in the United States of America

Book Cover Design by: Persist Marketing

Contents

Acknowledgements

Thank you to my friends and family that supported me through my business growth and through my journey writing this book. I know the amount of time I've poured into growing the business and writing the book came at the expense of your accessibility to me and I want to thank you for your love and patience. Not to sound cliché, but... I want to thank my momma lol. I want to thank my dad, my husband, my kids DeRiyah and Dj, my brothers, my friends, my clients, my team, my business besties, and most importantly... I want to thank God. Without him none of this would have been possible.

Introduction

Thank you for trusting me to help you in your career journey. Before we jump in, I want to give you some context as to why this book is so important. A lot of what I will share is information "they" won't tell you. Who is "they"? White corporate America. So, as you move through this book, highlight, add notations, circle, and underline your heart out because the objective is to move you out of a place of simply "surviving" and doing "ok", to thriving.

Before I move into the first play of thriving while black, understand a few key points:

- Oftentimes companies are looking for diversity simply to check a box so that they can be compliant with the EEOC requirements (but we knew that already).
- Most of you reading this book either identify with this next statement or you know someone who personally can-- black professionals are usually the ones who are picking up the slack at work and white leaders know it. But, because you don't assert your value, they choose to ignore it.

- While it costs the company to replace you, it also will cost to lose you. If you know how you bring the company or your department money, you then will become an asset, but again they won't tell you that.
- Those who want to support black and brown employees oftentimes don't know how to support.
- If you're waiting for the system to change, you're playing yourself. Play the game to win versus simply participating and waiting.

In order to thrive as a black professional in white corporate America (and really any workspace), you have to plan, strategize, and hold yourself accountable to bring the strategic plan to life. I would be lying if I didn't tell you that while having allies and accomplices are useful resources, there are strategies you can employ to manifest your growth on your terms. There is one main learning outcome I aim to achieve at the end of your reading: You will be able to understand how your MVP (Most Valuable Proposition) will position you as the MVP (Most Valuable Professional). Ok, let's get to it.

Play 1: Career Strategizing – The Basics

Professionals will often plan for their careers, but they don't strategize how to execute that plan. A person will plan to move from being an entry-level human resource professional to eventually becoming a chief human resource officer. The problem with this plan is, the person who is creating the plan has not strategized different pathways and actions needed to becoming a Chief Human Resource Officer. In order to successfully navigate career growth, black and brown professionals must understand that career growth is not always linear. It is a fluid process that sometimes involves pivoting and many times involves contingencies. You can be in a role that may not seem like it directly aligns to your desired career goal, but the key is knowing how to translate what you do into the role that you're aspiring to achieve.

Another key point to know when career strategizing is that you need a plan that includes contingencies. Sometimes there will be curve balls throughout your career and you need to have multiple routes to get to your goal. If you're adamant on taking one route, you'll set yourself up for failure. This was the first consistent challenge I noticed when coaching clients early on—the notion that there was one path to get to their desired career. When I realized so many black professionals consciously and unconsciously operated under this notion, I knew there was a lot of work needed in our community. This type of closed-minded thinking will cause career paralysis. To avoid career paralysis, be open and willing to strategically pivot when needed so that you maintain control of your career trajectory. Career strategizing is most effective when you understand how to use your value proposition. I created a model and a formula that has helped over 1100 black and brown professionals grow within their careers. Rest assured, I'm going to give you insight on my MVP formula later in the next chapter.

NOTES

_____

_____

_____

_____

_____

_____

_____

_____

_____

_____

_____

_____

_____

_____

_____

_____

_____

_____

NOTES

Play 2: Creating Your MVP

Now MVP stands for two things for me: Most Valuable Proposition and Most Valuable Professional. I like to have clients and professionals formulate their value proposition using my MVP formula. When you have the most valuable proposition formula applied correctly, you then become the most valuable professional. So when it comes down to understanding how to strategize your career as a black professional, you want to incorporate this formula in order to move past some of the systemic barriers in corporate America.

The main purpose of the MVP Formula is to position yourself as an asset. When you know how you're an asset, you are able to leverage opportunities and unfavorable situations so you're not just surviving in your career but you're thriving in it. Now let's take a deeper look at the value proposition formula.

The value proposition formula is as follows:
what you do (the task) and why it's important
+
who is impacted (that could be your department, that could be another department, that could be the entire company)
+
The quantified results (captured by how much, how often, and how many)
=
Most Valuable Proposition

When you use this formula and apply it to every aspect of your experiences, you will be able to begin constructing valuable propositions which then brands as a significant asset in your industry. Now when you think about this formula, the easiest way to apply it is by looking at your resume and applying it to each responsibility you have listed. As you do this throughout your resume, you'll begin to view your role a lot differently. From there, you'll understand how to articulate how you're an asset and you'll approach opportunities in a new way. You will have a better understanding of how you help/have helped companies save money, make money, save time, optimize processes, and overall, grow the business. Knowing how you're an asset moves you out of survival mode because you don't have to put up with crap at companies just for the sake of it. You can better establish boundaries and triggers that will activate different phases of your career strategy as you see fit. That means no more sitting around staying in positions because you're "waiting" for something to still open up after working there for 7+ years. That also means, giving leaders a run for their money when it comes down to choosing a candidate for a new role or promotional opportunity. Now if you're facing a hiring manager looking to maintain the systemic oppression, they have to decide between "green"(making/saving money) and white, versus "black and white".

NOTES

NOTES

NOTES

Play 3: Strategizing For Promotions

How many fellow black professionals do you know who will create a timeline and plan for when they want/need a promotion (who actually sticks to it and includes triggers)? I'll tell you right now, there aren't enough. Internal promotions can be tricky but that's why you need triggers built into your career strategy. Triggers are actions (or lack thereof) that are built into your career plan as indicators when you'll make a move within your plan.

For example, one part of your plan may include receiving a promotion within two years at your new company. A strategy for achieving that part of the plan may include winning employee of the year and exceeding certain metrics for your department. The trigger can be, if you don't receive the promotion, you'll begin searching for different opportunities (depending on the circumstance around not receiving the promotion). Or the trigger can be looking at a different internal opportunity. Regardless of the trigger, it's important that you have milestones in place that you plan to achieve within your role at a company to help you plan for the promotion. You should always go into a new role planning for the next step so that each day is intentional. With that being said, here are five strategies to consider when planning for promotions:

1. Track your achievements and metrics with day to day work tasks and projects. At the end of the book, there's an example of how to create a simple achievement tracker that you can plug in metrics you've achieved on a daily/weekly/monthly basis. Tracking your achievements and metrics are important because it allows you to create the narrative for performance review discussions, and it minimizes the chances of you forgetting about projects when it's time to discuss performance.

2. Prepare a needs analysis for the desired role at least a year in advance if possible. The needs analysis will compare what experience and skills will be needed to be qualified for the next desired role. This way, you ensure you're highly qualified.

3. Understand how you would make the (new) supervisor's job easier. This does not mean you're finding ways you can overwork yourself or suck up to any particular person. This is thinking strategically about what you can enhance within the scope of your work to provide some ease or

relief in a specific area for a future supervisor. When you can articulate your plans for the desired role to the person you would report to and it includes how you can make their job a bit easier--- that helps establish buy-in. This is not to say go over your own supervisor's head to get to a different opportunity per se, but to network internally and have organic conversations with intention.

4. Get your replacement ready. Already know who would be a viable replacement to make your transition out as smooth as possible. Companies view internal promotions very strategically. If you're too vital in a particular role, it's less risky for them to just bring in an outside person (in many cases) for that promotional role you wanted versus trying to find someone to fill a void you'd leave by being promoted. Of course you want to shine in your current role. However, if you know you do not plan to be in that role long term, you should be schooling someone on what you're doing so that they are somewhat groomed to come in and fill the void when you're promoted.

5. Go into performance evaluations with points you plan to discuss based on the direction you want the evaluation to go. You set the pace and the tone. Provide your supervisor with key accomplishments and achievements in advance to help them prepare

as well. Sometimes performance evaluations are informal and not structured with real accountability from senior leaders, so you need to make sure you're documenting everything that you're doing within your role. There are also biases that LIVE in the performance evaluation process. Those biases typically do not work in our favor. Knowing some of the biases that exist can help you maintain control of the conversation as well as help you come prepared to discuss your achievements and position any shortcomings (avoid spending a lot of time on this) as learning experiences. Some common biases include:

a. Shifting Standards- Shifting the criteria for rating based on who's being evaluated

b. Confirmatory Bias- Evaluating someone based on pre-existing beliefs about that person, ignoring information that proves otherwise

c. Recency Effect- rating someone based on something that recently happened versus looking at the entire history of time being evaluated

d. Primacy Effect- rating someone solely based on something that occurred early on. This is usually based on a mistake or unfavorable encounter.

While these strategies have proven to be instrumental in achieving promotions, sometimes the biggest hinderance is our own imposter syndrome. Feeling like we don't deserve to be in the spaces we most certainly deserve to be in. Before applying any of these strategies—do a self-check and be sure you go into evaluations with unwavering confidence and knowing what you deserve.

NOTES

Play 4: How to Strategize During a Job Search

Planning for a promotion and performance evaluation is one thing. Planning for an external job search is in another. There are a lot of areas that overlap such as, you need to do your research, you need to track your achievements and performance metrics, you need to know your value proposition, and you need to network. The biggest difference is honestly how you go about executing your strategy. Job searching can easily become depressing, but you have to be sure you're not job searching like it's 1999 and job search like we're in 2021. Those outdated steps of applying to a bunch of job postings on 3rd party sites and waiting for someone to call you is NO MORE. For a small select few, that still works. For the majority—especially blacks, that's a recipe for "not getting hired". Now let me be clear, if you're looking for an entry level role, or a high turnover role, you can sometimes be successful simply by applying and waiting for a callback.

If you're looking for mid-level leadership roles and higher, you need a strategy. Here are five steps to help you strategize your job search:

1. **Know your value proposition**. Your value proposition will help you position yourself as an asset. When you apply the MVP formula to all aspects of your job experiences, you're able to create an overarching value proposition for your professional brand. Your value proposition can adjust and outright change depending on the types of roles for which you will be applying.

2. **Be specific**. Your career documents and online brand need to be curated for the type of roles for which you are going to apply. There is no one size fits all resume/cover letter/LinkedIn profile. You need to brand yourself in alignment to the type of roles you'll be applying for and those roles need to be in the same job family. You can't use a Finance Manager resume to apply for IT roles.

3. **Use LinkedIn.** LinkedIn is a powerful, invaluable tool. This is my top tool for serious job seekers. LinkedIn really helps you job search smarter—not harder. LinkedIn allows you to position yourself as an expert in your space by providing multiple ways to share relevant content. Corporate leaders and hiring managers spend a great deal of time on

LinkedIn to learn insights from thought leaders and to find the next best thing in talent. When using LinkedIn to apply for jobs, you can access the job posters information, make contact with company leaders, and you can see how you match up to certain roles based on your experience and the requirements for the job. There are also online community groups that you can network in, learn from, and discover opportunities through.

4. **Conduct informational interviews.** Informational interviews are like secret weapons that many don't know about—at least not the type of informational interviews I educate my clients about. Informational interviews are an opportunity for you to speak with a senior leader in either a role you aspire to someday, a senior leader at a company you desire to work for, or a senior leader that can leverage their network for you to help with your career growth and job search. When done correctly, you can create a network of advocates who will mention your name in rooms you wouldn't otherwise be able to access. The main objective when you reach out to request an informational interview is to learn about the person's impressive career journey. Let them know your interest in wanting to grow in your career and that you'd appreciate if they could spare a

few minutes to share their journey. What happens during these calls typically is the leader gets an opportunity to "toot their horn" and share their story to the top (the good, bad, and ugly). What happens though toward the end of the calls, is they will ask you about your background and what exactly you're looking to achieve—boom! There it is, your chance to sell yourself! This is where your Most Value Proposition will make you the Most Valuable Professional. From there, they will either have bought into your story and how you're an asset in your field, or at a minimum, appreciate you reaching out and give you advice or recommendations to help you on your journey. If the leader you meet with has bought into you professionally, they'll look for opportunities to get you to your desired career goal without you even asking---BUT, be prepared to share how they can help you if they ask. Never simply reply "I don't know" to a question about how someone can help you. That's why you should have a career plan and strategy that is always evolving as you evolve.

5. **Research + Follow up.** Do your research. I repeat, DO YOUR RESEARCH! Information is at our fingertips nowadays. There is no reason you can't find out about a company's strategic plan, goals, upcoming priorities/initiatives, etc. Stop

going into these interviews ill-prepared. When you can connect your responses to interview questions to things currently happening within the company, you're showing the interviewer you're in a different league. You're showing them you did not come to play! Have intentional and impactful questions ready to ask as well. Research is key! It takes a little work, especially if you're like me and create a strategy around how you're going to use the information you found in your interview. But it's worth it. That's how I close my B2B clients when I get contracts to consult with different companies. Lastly—follow up. You're missing out on an opportunity to have your resume reviewed above the other 200+ applicants. Don't stalk hiring managers of course, but timely follow ups are needed.

NOTES

Play 5: Negotiate Like Your Life Depended On it

I'm going to say this once and only once--- STOP ACCEPTING THE FIRST THING COMPANIES OFFER! When companies are budgeting for hiring, the budget for salaries is usually a range. Now from a business perspective, do you think they are offering people the highest part of their salary budget?? In most cases, no. Then, let's add on this ingrained notion that black professionals can be paid less than white professionals to do identical jobs. With that being said, you KNOW they are most likely offering you the lower end of the budget and sadly, many black professionals just accept the offer. This happens for various reasons, such as fear of the offer being rescinded, not knowing how to negotiate, not knowing if you can be paid more, and the worse--- not recognizing you're being low balled because you went so long being underpaid.

This is why researching is so important. Learning salary schedules/company averages, promotion schedules, salary averages for the industry, and averages for your geographic area based on your industry is critical. This way you go into negotiation conversations with context of what a reasonable salary should be. Even with that, have your desired number ready and your case for why you are expecting that amount. Hint, hint, this ties back to your value proposition and how you're an asset. You need to be prepared to connect your value proposition to issues that are important to the company if needed. Are you seeing how everything ties back to your value proposition? I hope so.

Another important thing to note about negotiations is that when more black professionals negotiate and get paid what they really deserve, we begin to chip away at the racial wage gap and we slowly dismantle the notion that we can be paid less than our white counterparts. As we close the racial wage gap, we begin to close the racial wealth gap too. Oftentimes black households struggle to establish wealth because of a lack of discretionary funds to generate additional revenue streams. When we can make enough to cover monthly living expenses and savings, then we can begin investing (in a business, stocks, real estate, etc) to start building wealth. You see how negotiating is much bigger than you. It affects your family, your lineage, and the entire community. Of course, when making more money, a person must be disciplined and knowledgeable on investment endeavors, but you get the gist.

I already mentioned imposter syndrome earlier in the book and how it affects the performance evaluation process, but I want to remind you that it rears its ugly head when negotiation time approaches. When you can at least recognize it, you can fight through it. I still experience it during negotiations when discussing compensation with corporate B2B clients. Companies will see the results of my consulting with Fortune 500 and 250 companies and will still try to talk me down off my price when I've already researched what they pay their executive leaders and how they've allocated some of their financial resources so I KNOW they can afford my price point. I don't play that. They will put respect on my name and on those checks they write to me for my service. I need each of you reading this to vow that you will put respect on your name moving forward and make these companies put respect on your checks!

Lastly, when approaching any type of negotiation situation, don't just think about the salary as your only negotiating tool. Consider other compensation to negotiate such as PTO, work from home option, adjusted work schedule, professional development funds, stocks, an earlier performance review (this can be an opportunity to get a raise sooner than later after you've proved performance), as well as many other things.

NOTES

_____

_____

_____

_____

_____

_____

_____

_____

_____

_____

_____

_____

_____

_____

_____

_____

NOTES

Play 6: Supporting Research

The strategies outlined in this guide were influenced by informal and formal data collection. While many can see the racial disparities on the surface, I'm intentional in understanding the systems and unconscious behaviors that uphold racial disparities within the workplace. Before you start putting strategies into action, I encourage you to look at the data to understand the scope of what you're dealing with and many others that look like you.

According to a 2019 study done by the Center of Innovation (sponsored by Unilever, Disney, Danaher, Johnson & Johnson, Pzifer, and many others), it was found:

- While nearly two-thirds of black professionals agree they have to work harder than their colleagues to advance in their careers, very few white professionals see it that way. Most white professionals just aren't educated about, or aware of, this reality.

- Nearly half of white professionals feel they have access to senior leaders at work, while black professionals find that a line to top leadership is more elusive.
- Black professionals are more likely to encounter racial prejudice and microaggressions at work, than any other group.

What does all of this tell us? That black professionals have way more obstacles in front of them to get to the top (which we knew, but there's more data now to support it). This means we need to work smarter not harder. This is why I teach the MVP formula to become the MVP (Most Valuable Professional) as well as all the strategies outlined in this playbook in addition to many others. You have to use all your resources and be serious about advancement which includes recognizing that investing in yourself is a likely step to get over your hurdles quicker and more effectively.

Key Findings - BEING BLACK IN CORPORATE AMERICA (talentinnovation.org).

Additionally, a 2020 article by Forbes shows us that for career progression that aligns with securing a higher salary, it's not only about who you know and what you know, but it's about who knows you and what you're known for. This means you need to have a professional brand that ties you to the results of your work!

https://www.forbes.com/sites/danabrownlee/2020/10/08/dear-black-professionals-6-pieces-of-advice-a-white-manager-may-not-give-you/?sh=76483b3a3de1

Next Steps: Becoming the MVP (Most Valuable Professional)

I'm all about executing and having action steps after a conversation. After going over everything, I want to give you clear action steps to begin taking in order to implement these strategies.

- Leave a review sharing how this playbook was beneficial to you (now you should have known there was going to be a shameless plug, lol)
- If you didn't, go back and highlight the areas you need to address most. Make it easy to find the information you need most when you're ready to apply it
- Start with your resume. Look it over and ask yourself "do I look like a high value asset?" If not— get to work rebranding yourself professionally, starting with the resume
  - Tip: Remove the identifiable info on your resume and ask a colleague/friend to give their first thoughts when they glance at the document for a few seconds
  - Depending on how serious you are about growing your career and moving out of five-figure roles and into six-figure roles, consider a professional career coach and/or resume

writer to help you flush out your brand and capture it as effectively as possible. Career coaching is NOT a luxury expense, it's a strategic investment in which you should anticipate ROI

- Assess where your skills/experience gaps are and look for projects or professional development opportunities where you can bridge those gaps
- Brand your LinkedIn profile to reflect where you're trying to go in your career (similar to your resume)
- Network (LinkedIn makes this easy) to build yourself a tribe of like-minded individuals to keep you focused and motivated on your career growth. You want people around you who that are working towards growth, who can challenge you and hold you accountable
- Network with senior and executive leaders who can help you align yourself with opportunities. Informational interviews can make the networking process a little less daunting in my opinion
- Reach out to the E3 Professional Services team, www.e3-proservices.com , if you want 1:1 help with demonstrating how you're the MVP (Most Valuable Professional) or schedule directly at https://bit.ly/e3consult

Now let's get to these wins!

NOTES

Bonus Chapter—Leverage Your Salary To Build Wealth (excerpt from Thriving and Black 2.0)

I've mentioned before that in the black community, the issue is not always the lack of education surrounding wealth and how to build it, it's often not having access to enough discretionary income to nurture additional streams of income. When I began to really educate myself on how people retire with boatloads of money, one thing remained consistent—it took money to generate additional streams of revenue. Then I looked at the different revenue streams for building wealth and realized each required some type of money/credit to get "skin in the game". Then my question was, how are black professionals supposed to have enough discretionary income to establish multiple income streams? The answer seemed simple--by increasing their income. But then the issue was, companies are offering low ball salaries and a lot of the black community is not well versed on how to negotiate salaries or even plan for strategic career growth. So many black Americans attend college, and we're taught how to get a "job", but there's no (or very little) strategic efforts educating college students about strategically growing in their careers: the importance of negotiating from DAY 1, how to negotiate, how to develop your value proposition, how to do a gap analysis of skills/experiences, how to develop confidence to advocate for oneself... the list could go on.

This is why so many black professionals in the workforce feel complacent and stuck in mid-management roles and are underpaid. We are undercutting ourselves from the start of our careers. But not anymore! I don't just want black professionals to earn higher salaries, I want them to know what to do with those salaries as they close the racial wage gap! It all starts with knowing your value proposition. The beauty about understanding your value proposition is you can apply it in every area of your life!

Achievement Tracker

Feel free to use this tracker to keep up with your impacts at work and awards/recognition/special projects. This helps when the time comes for bonuses, appraisal reviews, or even when you're ready for a new role. Feel free to tweak titles for the sections to best align with your industry.

Task/Project (include date if applicable)	How many/ How much (200 calls a day, 50 accounts managed, 10 staff members supervised)	Departments You collaborated (did you work with another dept. for this, if so who	Results (what is the ultimate outcome of you doing this. Does it help another dept? Remember it helps the company SOMEHOW! Think $, or numbers if possible	Other relevant information

Awards and Recognition

1.
2.
3.
4.
5.

Photo Credit: Marlon Womack

About the Author

DeAnnah Stinson Reese is a media featured, award nominated Career Strategist for Black Professionals and Global DEI Strategist for companies. As a Chicago native, she serves as CEO and Principal Consultant for E3 Professional Services. DeAnnah uses her 10+ years of combined experience in equitable hiring, retention, DEI education, and career development to change the game for how black professionals progress in their career. DeAnnah and her team educates, equips, and empowers black kings and queens to advance in their careers using her proprietary career strategizing model while also partnering with companies to diversify their leadership by creating more equitable workplace cultures.

As a corporate equity educator and DEI strategist, DeAnnah helps companies to understand the power of biases, privilege, race, and social injustices to strategize ways to cultivate diverse and inclusive workplaces with equitable opportunities which helps retain top diverse talent.

Thriving and Black: The Playbook came out of a pattern she noticed from coaching over 1000 professionals, which was-- many did not understand the value they bring as a professional and/or did not know how to convey that value in writing and during interviews. Many black professionals do not feel confident negotiating compensation and are hesitant to go after top leadership roles; but not after Thriving and Black!

DeAnnah has been fortunate to partner with Fortune 500 companies from Stanley Black and Becker to Microsoft and is looking forward to new partnerships with companies like Facebook and BET.

www.ingramcontent.com/pod-product-compliance
Lightning Source LLC
Chambersburg PA
CBHW070919210326
41521CB00010B/2249